IMAGES
of America

AROUND
SOMERSWORTH

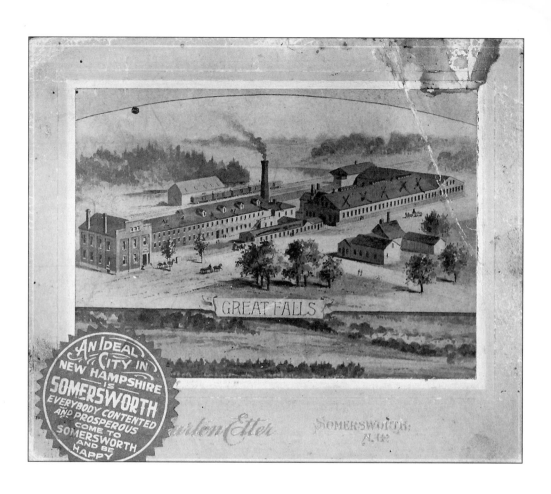

GREAT FALLS

AN IDEAL CITY IN NEW HAMPSHIRE IS SOMERSWORTH EVERYBODY CONTENTED AND PROSPEROUS COME TO SOMERSWORTH AND BE HAPPY

SOMERSWORTH N.H.

IMAGES
of America

AROUND
SOMERSWORTH

Compiled by
Frank Clark and MaryBeth Faucher
from the Collection of the Summersworth Historical Society

ARCADIA

Published by Arcadia Publishing,
an imprint of the Chalford Publishing Corporation,
One Washington Center, Dover, New Hampshire 03820.
Printed in Great Britain.

ISBN 0-7524-0094-0

Contents

Introduction

Somersworth is a mill city. Since 1823, the mills (especially the Great Falls Manufacturing Company) have been the single most important element in the growth, change in culture, and entire identity of Somersworth. But the history of Somersworth begins well before the Industrial Revolution.

Somersworth began as a parish of Dover known as Sligo, "doubtless so called from the town of that name in Ireland, 'Sligo town that lies so snug at the foot of Knocknaria" (*History of Stafford County*, 213). The name changed to Summersworth, meaning "summer town," because during the summer the ministers of Dover would preach there, so that all could attend. Ministers from Dover continued to preach there until 1729, when a separate parish was established, and a new, year-round minister was hired. The area continued to grow and became a town in 1754.

It was at this point that the spelling of the name changed to Somersworth, due to a mistake made on official documents. It is the only town with that name (spelled either way) in the United States and England. Until the early 1800s, the center of the town had always been in what is today Rollinsford Junction. As the mills grew the center of town moved upstream to the village of Great Falls and away from the old center of town. Conflict began between the "old" and the "new," resulting in the separation of the old and the formation of the separate town of Rollinsford in 1849.

At the time of this separation, it had been some twenty years since the textile mills were built and in that time the area that we know today as Somersworth began to take shape. Using the power of the falls the mills brought the Industrial Revolution to the banks of the Salmon Falls River. This growth would forever change the face of the city.

Like all New England mill towns, Somersworth's history is intertwined with the story of its mills. The mills required laborers, and soon people came here to earn a living, creating a new class of people with cash to spend and save. This created a need for merchants and businessmen. The Great Falls Bank and the Somersworth Savings Bank were established, and shops were opened. New roads were built to Dover where goods for the mills were received and sent. The entire region was enhanced by the religion, language, and culture brought by immigrants who came to work in Somersworth. Railroads came to town in 1842 and brought Boston businesses to within a mere three-hour trip, and forty years later trolleys brought public transportation to the common person. The area was described in 1840 by James Montgomery like this:

"This is one of the pleasantest and most beautiful manufacturing villages I have ever seen... Along the outside of the main street are the boarding houses or dwelling houses for the mill workers; these are neat brick buildings, three stories in height, and each building contains four tenements: there are seven of these boarding houses, set at equal distance from each other, which gives to the whole an appearance of neatness and uniformity. The main street, the canal, and the mills, are running in parallel lines with a large open area between them, and have a most delightful effect upon the mind of a stranger when he first enters the village. The whole plan of the village displays good taste, and its general appearance is delightful and beautiful in the highest degree."

This tremendous period of growth resulted in the establishment of the city in 1893, but there was a problem: what to call the new city? The area had always been known as Great Falls even though it had officially been a part of Somersworth. To add to the confusion, the post office, established in 1825, took the name of Great Falls; as a result, many people in town did not even know that they lived in Somersworth. The town council, however, did not want to be known as the City of Great Falls, so they returned to the name of Somersworth and the city has gone by that name ever since.

The city has changed a great deal from the early days of the mills. Trains and trolleys replaced horses and wagons, only to be replaced by cars and buses. The days of the five-and-ten have come and gone; bearskin coats and spats are no longer the style of the day; and there is no diner to be found in town. The textile mills have left the city, but the modern business of General Electric carries on the tradition of industry.

Over the years, Somersworth has been the workplace and playground, the schoolyard and living room, to thousands of people, and has touched the lives of thousands more. We hope that this book can bring a little bit of that history and some of those faces to life with a view of the past. We have gathered photographs that tell the history of Somersworth as it was seen by the people who lived in it. This book contains pictures, images that tell the story of a city, a community. But these images tell more than the story of the community: they also tell about a time, a time not long gone. We hope you have as much fun reading this as we did putting it together.

One

Downtown

Main Street, Market Street, and High Street are today, as they have always been, the center of downtown Somersworth. One hundred years ago or more "downtown" held a different meaning to residents than it does today. Today, when we need to go to the store or are looking for something to do in the evening, we can hop in our cars and very shortly be at the mall or in Boston. Former residents did not have this opportunity, however, and the downtown area had to supply all of their needs. It was here that you would find stores, transportation, entertainment, churches, meeting halls, banks, and commercial establishments.

As you look through these photographs, look closely at the dirt roads (some with trolley tracks and some without), the people, and the buildings (many of which are still standing, while others have long since disappeared); we bet you can picture yourself in this by-gone era.

An aerial view of downtown in the 1940s. Notice St. Martin's School and Church in the foreground and the prominent view of the mills: in the upper left are old textile mill buildings and in center is the General Electric plant. Beyond the clustered downtown is the very rural area of Berwick across the river.

A mid-1800s view of Main Street looking south. On the right is the Great Falls Hotel and down the street in the distance is the long row of brick boarding houses located across the street from the Great Falls Manufacturing Company. The mill is just out of the picture on the left.

An artists view of Market Street in the early 1800s. Single-story wooden and brick buildings, such as this one near the Berwick Bridge, were the homes of the early merchants of the town.

A stereoptic view of the Free Press building on Market Street. Local newspapers began as early as 1867 with the *Great Falls Journal* and the *Advertiser*. These merged with the Free Press in 1881 and continued to be the leading paper in Somersworth into the twentieth century.

The corner of Main and High Streets facing up High Street in the mid-1800s. In the foreground is a load of wood awaiting a purchaser. This square was a famous place for wood teams to congregate, during fall and winter mornings, from a distance of up to 20 miles to sell their latest harvest of logs. Somersworth was a great market for wood in the days of wood-burning locomotives, and before coal began to be used extensively in houses and businesses.

A view up High Street from corner of High and Elm Streets in the late 1800s. Notice the changes from the same view in the earlier photograph, including the trolley tracks and dirt road, the bandstand at the corner, and the expansion of the buildings on the right.

A 1908 postcard of High Street. The ingenious design of this postcard adds a birch bark border to give a touch of the woods to the city. Notice the absence of the bandstand. The building on the left is the Somersworth Savings Bank, built in 1876, and destroyed by fire in 1963.

Officers of the court in the 1920s. The court was located in the back of the town hall, which would later become the Opera House. Pictured are, from left to right: Attorney Sidney Stevens; Clerk of the Court Albert White; Judge Christopher Wells; and Police Chief Charles P. Andrews. Wells not only served as judge, but was also the publisher of the *Free Press*, which he purchased in the 1890s.

Main Street facing toward Market Street in the early 1900s. The B & M Railroad Station, which is still standing today, is the brick building up ahead on right; on the left is the Great Falls Hotel, built in 1825. In the background you can see the distinctive shape of the Great Falls National Bank.

A view of Main Street in the 1950s. This view was taken from the corner of Washington and Main at the Opera House, looking north. On the left are the mill company boarding houses. These were built in the nineteenth century to house mill workers, and they remained standing until the late 1960s when they were torn down for urban renewal. This area today is a parking lot for a shopping plaza.

The photograph above is an early-twentieth-century view of Sullivan Square, in downtown Berwick, Maine. The photograph on the right is of Sullivan Monument, which lies across the square from the gas station (pictured above). Revolutionary War General John Sullivan was born in Berwick, and his father was the first schoolmaster in Somersworth.

Other views of Sullivan Square. Since Berwick lies right across the bridge from downtown Somersworth, the two towns have always been closely connected. The large building with the cupola in the above picture is Grant's Hotel, a popular stopover for travelers from the mid-1800s into the early twentieth century.

The town hall of Berwick, Maine. Located where current fire station is, the town hall was the center for town meetings, where all residents of the town could come and voice their opinions. This democratic form of government still exists in many New England towns.

Downtown Rollinsford, New Hampshire, in 1955. This section of town was home to the Salmon Falls Manufacturing Company, which was incorporated about the same time as the Great Falls Mill, thus helping to move the center of Rollinsford away from Rollinsford Junction.

A view of High Street looking toward Market Street in the 1940s. The Memorial Hall Building is on the left and the former Congregational church can be seen further down the hill. This street scene remains virtually unchanged today (except the cars, of course).

"Everybody ate at Vic's." Formally Lothrup's, until it was sold to Vic Charpentier, this diner was a fixture in downtown near the mill. Vic's was located on Main Street across from the present location of the library.

An early view of Market Street businesses. Looking at this same location today would show a much different downtown, with more modern buildings replacing the wooden ones. In the background we can see Berwick, with Grant's Hotel on the left.

The Great Falls National Bank. Incorporated as Great Falls Bank in 1846, it became Great Falls National Bank in 1865. The building sits on the site of an old blacksmith shop constructed to build tools and machines for the early mills. Erected in 1846, with the second story added in 1874, it was home to the bank until 1965. Today it is home to Pearl's Bakery.

Views of Somersworth and Sullivan Square "in the future." Two of a number of such postcards from the early years of this century, they show what must have been common expectations for the future, based on the technology of the day. Such expectations included the construction of a subway to New York, an elevated train to Boston, and zeppelin and balloon travel.

Two

The Mills

The Great Falls Manufacturing Company was founded in 1822 by Isaac Wendell, a Quaker from Boston. Little did he know what a pronounced affect his company would have on the town and the region. In its formative years, Wendell served as agent and oversaw the daily operations of his mill. What follows is an account by Wendell's daughter, relating a humorous tale of the mill's beginnings:

"No intoxicating drink was allowed on the place, while under my father's control...but liquor was often secretly obtained. The laborers building the walls of the canal, left little hiding places for the bottle. Father had no control in Maine and the men sent their shoes to be mended, he thought, rather oftener than was necessary, and one day, observing a messenger boy returning with a pair of boots, he approached the boy on the bridge, but before they met, the boots went over the railing into the river, and the story was told." (*History of Strafford County*)

The Great Falls Manufacturing Company with a canal and train in foreground, in the late 1800s. The river on the other side of the mills drops 100 feet over the course of a mile; this canal brought water to the mills to power the water wheels in the basements. The railroad made possible the transportation of raw materials and products. This photograph shows the early buildings of the mill as well as the bell tower essential to keeping schedules in the mill.

A woman sitting at her desk with an elephant statue and cloth carts. The bulk of people employed in the mills were women, who performed a variety of tasks. Not all work in the mills was machine work; business needed to be attended to as well. Note the visible pipes and cloth in the room. We're not sure about the elephant.

Spinning room workers *c.* 1915. Posed group shots were common in the mills, and make up the bulk of all remaining mill photos. As in many photos, the workers are posed around the overseer and/or agent. In this room the cotton fibers were spun into thread and put onto bobbins to be woven. Most work in the mill was dirty, noisy, and difficult. If you look closely at this picture you can see the cotton dust covering the workers. Also note the different condition of the agent seated in the center.

Another view of a spinning room in the 1920s. Note the different style of dress and hair. A closer look also shows electric lights in the picture, but there is still cotton on the floor. There may also be a sense of sisterhood here, as shown by the workers with their arms around each other.

GREAT FALLS MANUFACTURING COMPANY.

Counting Room, _____ June 13 1853.

The name of _____ Susan Van Deen _____ is registered for No. 2 _____ Weaving _____ Room. W. C. L.

GENERAL REGULATIONS.

All persons in the employ of the Great Falls Manufacturing Company are requested to be punctual and constant in their attendance during the hours of labor and not to be absent from work without consent, excepting in cases of sickness, and then immediate information is to be sent to the overseer.

All persons in the employ of the Company will be considered as agreeing to work as many hours each day, and for each and every day's work, as the mills were usually run prior to the fifteenth day of September, 1847.

Any person intending to leave the Company's employ must give notice to his or her overseer two weeks at least previous to leaving, and continue to work till the expiration of the notice.— Those who leave contrary to this regulation, sickness excepted, will not be settled with or paid, till such notice is regularly given and worked out. The foregoing regulations will be regarded as an express contract between the corporation and all persons in its employ; and all who continue to work for the corporation will be considered as agreeing to the terms here stated, particularly those relating to the hours of labor and notice of leaving.

Transfers of help from one room or mill to another, will be regulated exclusively by the overseers.

Any person who may take from the mills, shops or yards, any of the Company's property without leave, will be considered as guilty of stealing, and punished accordingly.

Reading, sewing and knitting cannot be permitted in the mills.

Females will be required to board on the corporation, excepting those who board with their Parents, Brother or Sister.

All persons in the employ of the Company are positively required to abstain from the use of ardent spirits as a beverage.

Profanity and indecent language cannot be permitted in the mills.

All persons in the employ of this Company are earnestly advised to attend public worship on the Sabbath.

Any person guilty or believed to be guilty of immoral, improper or disorderly conduct, will be discharged.

J. A. BURLEIGH, AGENT.

Some general regulations of the Great Falls Manufacturing Company in 1853. Workers in the mill were governed in their lives as well as their work. As seen here, they were required to live in company-owned boarding houses and "earnestly advised" to attend public worship on the Sabbath. There were prohibitions against the use of profanity and "ardent spirits," and one of the regulations decreed that "any person guilty or believed to be guilty of immoral, improper or disorderly conduct, will be discharged." By 1826 the first dwellings owned by the company were completed: forty dwellings of wood, five extensive boarding houses, five brick blocks, three stores, and a great number of buildings occupied by mechanics.

The spool room of Mill #3. This scene seems to be from about the time of the earlier spinning room photographs (on p.25). Notice that once again the agent is present. Though the workers seem to be less dirty they also seem younger. The mills were run by water and power was sent to rooms by leather belts and pulleys: just behind these workers can be seen some very large belts, with smaller belts to run individual machines further in the background.

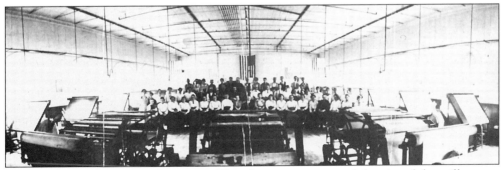

A mill room in the twentieth century. This shot gives a sense of the size of the mill rooms, which had large windows for light. The machines in the foreground were used for inspecting frames for the cloth. Note the many flags in the room.

Making "roving" at Salmon Falls Manufacturing Company Mill #2. There are many steps in the production of cotton (or wool) cloth. The raw cotton must be carded or combed and the fibers drawn out before being spun into thread. Roving is one of the many steps in this process.

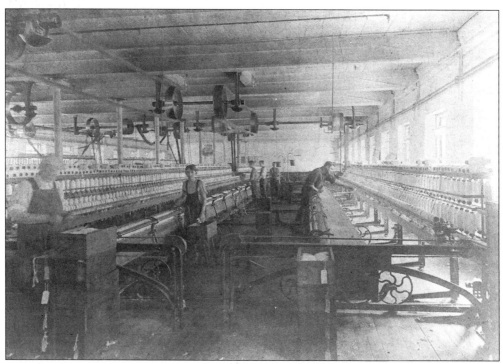

A mule spinning room in 1912. Mule spinning was a skilled process for spinning thread, primarily reserved for male workers: on the left is Richard Mason, second hand; in the center, Oliver Bisson; and on right, leaning over, is Emile Boucher.

A General Electric production line in the mid-twentieth century. This automated production line is the modern version of the mill. Here we see workers assembling electric meters.

The interior of the General Electric plant. The modern factory has much more machinery and technological equipment then its older predecessors. With more advanced technology, fewer people were needed to run more and more machines.

A machine shop in the late 1800s. The operation of the mills required a constant supply of machine parts and tools. These machinists were among the most highly skilled workers in the mills. The high-tech tools of the day still seems very basic to us, especially when compared to the technology of the computer age.

The Somersworth Foundry at Salmon Falls. The foundry was established shortly after the mills began operation. Not only was iron for the mills produced here, but it also supplied iron to Strafford and York Counties. Manufacturing stoves was also a specialty.

A twentieth-century shoe factory. Shoe manufacturing began in the city as early as 1885. In the twentieth century, shoe shops also could be found in former textile mills. Here you can see US Senator Thomas McIntyre and his city chairperson, Elizabeth Ball, visiting a Somersworth shoe shop to seek support.

The Great Falls Bleachery and Dye-Works. The bleachery was built in 1852 under the Burliegh administration and by 1891 was listed among the leading bleacheries in the country. Notice the railroad lines running along the building for ease in loading and unloading, making the most efficient use of space possible.

Great Falls Bleachery and Dye-Works workers in 1937, also known as the Dye-House Gang. Shown here are, from left to right: (front) Leo Cater, Joe Cliche, Whitey Nolan, Lucien Chasse, Joseph Aubert, Gerard Chasse, George Bickford, Al Dionne, Edward McGuinness, and G. Gaudette; (back) George Dumont, Gideon Doyon, Veris Turcotte, Harry Ricker, Albert Hersey, Gideon Doyon, Stony Turmelle, Joseph Leper (the head dyer), Leo Labonte, Roderick St. Laurent, Roland Gauvin, Del Lessard, Sydney McNally, and William Ricker.

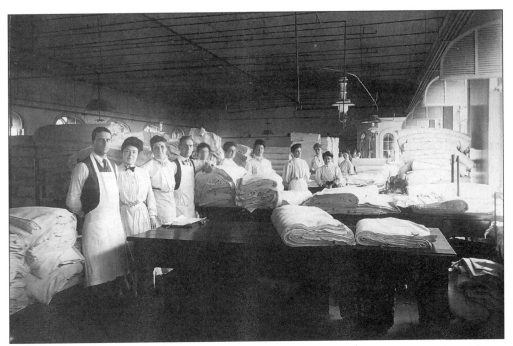

A cloth room of the Great Falls Manufacturing Company. The Great Falls Manufacturing Company turned out thirteen different kinds of cloth, specializing in drillings, shirtings, and sheetings. The cloth shown here appears to have already been bleached and the workers are all dressed in white. It was in this room that the cloth was prepared for shipment. Notice the age of the overhead gas lamps.

An advertising card of the Great Falls Bleachery. Textile mills often had labels that were shipped out with their goods to distinguish them from the many other New England companies. This scene shows the contrast between popular pastoral views and the industry of the city.

Mill #3 of the Great Falls Manufacturing Company. Early mills were built with a effort to include greenspace within the mill complex. These "malls" could have been used by the workers for Sunday strolls, and helped ease the change from rural to industrial life.

Mill #3, with a canal, in winter. This shows the same area during the winter, with an excellent view of the canals and footbridges, contrasted against the snow. As time went on the mills needed to supplement water power with steam power, as evidenced here by the smokestack in the background.

The building of the new mill on July 20, 1920. This photograph shows the same area as the previous two photographs, but from the other direction. Construction is underway for a new mill building. With steam power and electricity, mills no longer had to be built along the canals, and land became too valuable to remain undeveloped. Modern construction gave these new mills a different look than the old brick buildings.

The General Electric plant in the 1950s. The construction of 1920 produced a building that would have several lives. In 1929 the power rights of the Great Falls Manufacturing Company were sold to the Public Service Company of New Hampshire. The Nashua Manufacturing Company took over in 1932, but the building was vacant for several years before World War II, when the US Government took it over. Repairs and improvements to the building were made and the electrical department from the Portsmouth Naval Shipyard was eventually transferred here. In 1947 General Electric moved in and began producing electrical meters here.

The storehouse, cloth hall, #2 picker, and #2 mill. The term "mill" did not always refer to a single building, but could also refer to the whole complex of buildings used in the production of cloth. The most interesting element of this photograph is the unique shape of the storehouse in the foreground. The small windows indicate that this building was not used for work and did not need much light. Early mill workrooms built before electricity needed to make the best use of window light for work.

The mills as seen from the east side of the river. The neat, orderly appearance of the front of the mills hides a different view from behind. In the foreground we see the tailraces from the mill, where the water re-enters the river after turning the wheels of the mill. This jumble of buildings shows that a lot was going on behind the scenes.

The fire in Mill #2 on September 8, 1930. One member of the Somersworth Historical Society described it like this:

"My mother came into our room and woke us up, it was the middle of the night. She wrapped us up in a blanket and we watched the fire from our bedroom window. The window looked out over a grove of trees to the mill beyond. The flames were shooting way up into the sky. After, I heard that our house was saved because it had a slate roof, because the sparks were blowing that way. It was scary. In the last few years I have realized that my mother wanted us [the two oldest] awake in case we had to leave the house, so we could help with the younger children."

The new dam. Located downstream from the Great Falls Manufacturing Company and the bridge to Berwick, this was the former site of the original grist and saw mills in town, and later the location of the Great Falls Woolen Company. Today this is near the present wastewater treatment plant.

The Great Falls Woolen Company at the new dam. During the Civil War the cotton mills were shut down due to the lack of cotton from the South. The local answer for this was the building of the Great Falls Woolen Company in 1863, which supplied Army goods during the war. It was still in operation into the early years of this century.

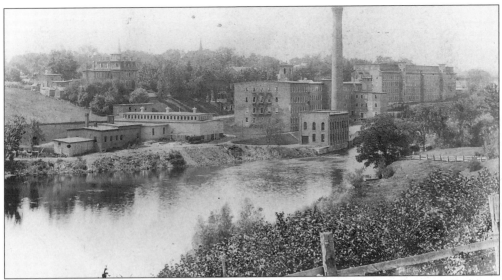

The Salmon Falls Mills as seen from downstream. The Salmon Falls Manufacturing Company was established in Rollinsford on June 17, 1822. Although these mills were established at the same time as the Great Falls mills they were never as large. The counting house (on the left in the bottom photo) was the business center of the mills. Here the bookkeepers, agents, and other management personnel worked. In many of the early mills, once the morning bell was rung, the gates were locked, and all those late for work had to walk through the counting house to be checked in.

Officers of the Great Falls Manufacturing Company at the turn of the century. Included in this photograph are: (top row, at the far left) Agent Charles Plummer; (top row, fourth from the left) Cy Freeman, overseer of the cloth hall from 1870 to 1914; and (top row, fourth from the right) Harry Campbell, who was the last veteran of the Spanish-American War residing in Somersworth.

A cloth-room woman of the late 1800s. This is one of our favorite pictures. We think it speaks for itself...

Three
Residential and Rural

As the mill and the town grew and the population expanded, there was an increased demand for places to live and schools for the area's children. Beyond downtown Somersworth was a whole other side to the city, where mills gave way to houses and, further on, to rolling hills and farms.

Although the mill was the single most important element in town and the downtown area offered excitement and entertainment, the residential and rural areas were where many people spent the majority of their time. To them, the "country," which was such a short distance from Main Street, was home; here, the presence of the mills, felt so strongly in town, was nowhere to be found.

Tate's Brook in 1907. On the back of this postcard was written, "Who said we didn't have some pretty spots in Somersworth? What's the matter with this place?" Just like most New England mill towns once you left downtown you entered a quiet, rural world perfect for riding and strolls.

The largest elm in the United States. On the farm of Albert C. Ham at Crockett's Crossing on Main Street was located this nationally renowned tree. In 1922, it was estimated to be 300 years old, 100 feet high, and 25 feet in circumference.

Aerial views from the high school tower. These two photographs were taken from the old high school tower around the turn of the century, looking toward the downtown area. In the top view the mill is to the right, while in the bottom view the same mill is to the left. The cluster of buildings to the far left in the top picture is the town of Berwick; in the bottom photograph Main Street, Somersworth, is directly ahead.

A rural mail carrier at the turn of the century. Pictured here is Pierre Paradis, rural mail carrier (RR1), making a delivery to a farm on Stackpole Road. The mail delivery and railroads linked people to the outside world.

A horse and wagon. Looking toward town from the cracker factory beyond Horne Street, Old Holy Trinity Church can be seen in the mid-distance. No sign can be seen of the many houses that are now just a few short blocks from Main Street.

For all those residents who lived beyond the downtown area, horse-drawn wagons were still the main access to town and the shops and entertainment there. Wagons were also used by merchants and peddlers to make deliveries and sell their wares. Within a decade of these photographs, electric trolleys would make travel faster and easier.

Schoolchildren outside Burliegh School with flags and baskets, *c.* 1923.

The first grade class of Burliegh School in 1914.

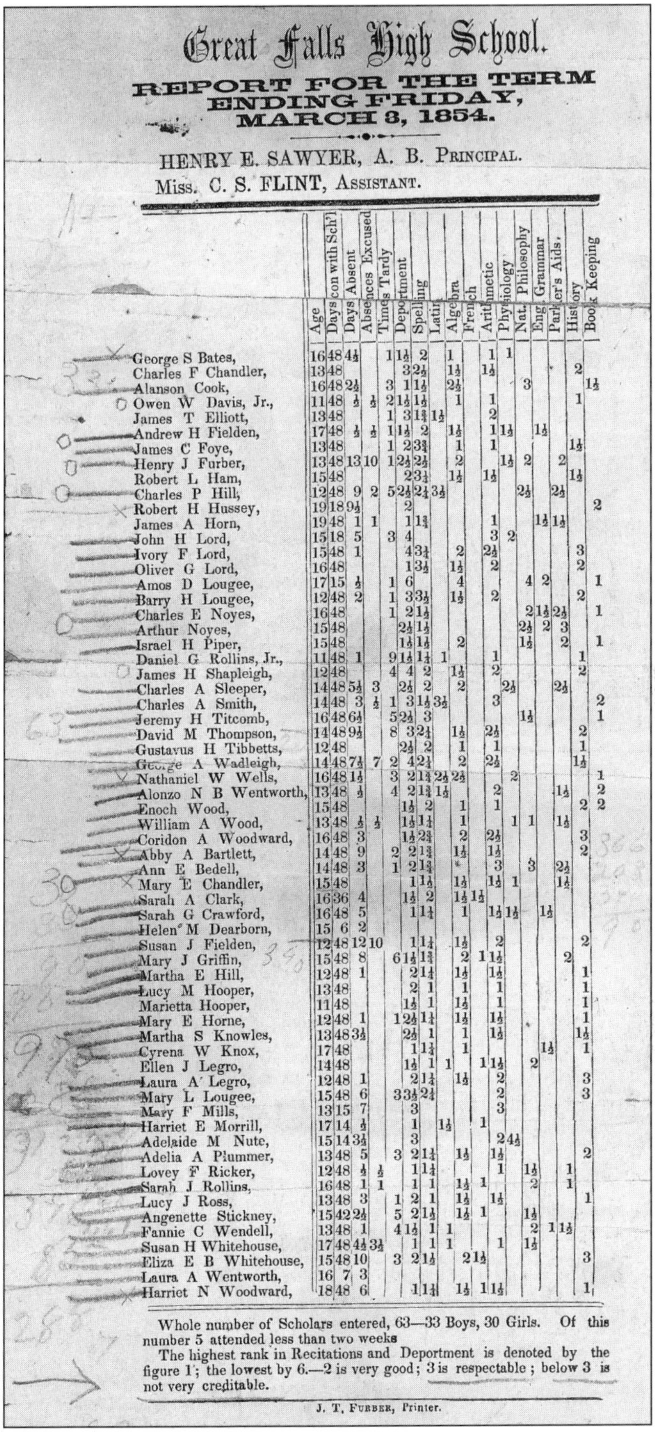

Great Falls High School.

REPORT FOR THE TERM ENDING FRIDAY, MARCH 3, 1854.

HENRY E. SAWYER, A. B. PRINCIPAL.
Miss. C. S. FLINT, ASSISTANT.

	Age	Days con with Sch'l	Days Absent	Absences Excused	Times Tardy	Deportment	Spelling	Latin	Algebra	French	Arithmetic	Physiology	Nat. Philosophy	Eng. Grammar	Parker's Aids.	History	Book Keeping
George S Bates,	16	48	4½		1	1½	2		1		1	1					
Charles F Chandler,	13	48				3	2½		1½		1½					2	
Alanson Cook,	16	48	2½		3	1	1½		2½				3				1½
Owen W Davis, Jr.,	11	48	½	½	2	1½	1½		1		1					1	
James T Elliott,	13	48			1	3	1¾	1½			2						
Andrew H Fielden,	17	48	½	½	1	1½	2		1½		1	1½		1½			
James C Foye,	13	48			1	2	3¾		1		1					1½	
Henry J Furber,	13	48	13	10	1	2½	2½		2			1½	2		2		
Robert L Ham,	15	48				2	3¼		1½		1½					1½	
Charles P Hill,	12	48	9	2	5	2½	2¼	3½					2½		2½		
Robert H Hussey,	19	18	9½			2											2
James A Horn,	19	48	1	1		1	1¾				1			1½	1½		
John H Lord,	15	18	5		3	4					3	2					
Ivory F Lord,	15	48	1			4	3¼		2		2½					3	
Oliver G Lord,	16	48				1	3½		1½		2					2	
Amos D Lougee,	17	15	½		1	6			4				4	2			1
Barry H Lougee,	12	48	2		1	3	3½		1½		2					2	
Charles E Noyes,	16	48			1	2	1½						2	1½	2½		1
Arthur Noyes,	15	48				2½	1½						2½	2	3		
Israel H Piper,	15	48				1½	1½		2				1½		2		1
Daniel G Rollins, Jr.,	11	48	1		9	1½	1¼	1			1					1	
James H Shapleigh,	12	48			4	4	2		1½		2					2	
Charles A Sleeper,	14	48	5½	3		2½	2		2			2½			2½		
Charles A Smith,	14	48	3	½	1	3	1½	3½			3						2
Jeremy H Titcomb,	16	48	6½		5	2½	3						1½				1
David M Thompson,	14	48	9½		8	3	2¼		1½		2½					2	
Gustavus H Tibbetts,	12	48				2½	2		1		1					1	
George A Wadleigh,	14	48	7½	7	2	4	2¼		2		2½					1½	
Nathaniel W Wells,	16	48	1½		3	2	1¾	2½	2½			2					1
Alonzo N B Wentworth,	13	48	½		4	2	1¾	1½			2				1½		2
Enoch Wood,	15	48				1½	2		1		1					2	2
William A Wood,	13	48	½	½		1½	1¼		1			1	1		1½		
Coridon A Woodward,	16	48	3			1½	2¾		2		2½					3	
Abby A Bartlett,	14	48	9		2	2	1¾		1½		1½					2	
Ann E Bedell,	14	48	3		1	2	1¾				3		3		2½		
Mary E Chandler,	15	48				1	1½		1½		1½	1			1½		
Sarah A Clark,	16	36	4			1½	2		1½	1½							
Sarah G Crawford,	16	48	5			1	1¼		1		1½	1½		1½			
Helen M Dearborn,	15	6	2														
Susan J Fielden,	12	48	12	10		1	1¼		1½		2					2	
Mary J Griffin,	15	48	8		6	1½	1¾		2	1	1½				2		
Martha E Hill,	12	48	1			2	1¼		1½		1½					1	
Lucy M Hooper,	13	48				2	1		1		1					1	
Marietta Hooper,	11	48				1½	1		1½		1					1	
Mary E Horne,	12	48	1		1	2½	1¼		1½		1½					1	
Martha S Knowles,	13	48	3½			2½	1		1		1½					1½	
Cyrena W Knox,	17	48				1	1¼		1					1½		1	
Ellen J Legro,	14	48				1½	1	1		1	1½		2				
Laura A Legro,	12	48	1			2	1¼		1½		2					3	
Mary L Lougee,	15	48	6		3	3½	2¼				2					3	
Mary F Mills,	13	15	7			3					3						
Harriet E Morrill,	17	14	½			1		1½		1							
Adelaide M Nute,	15	14	3½			3					2	4½					
Adelia A Plummer,	13	48	5		3	2	1¼		1½		1½					2	
Lovey F Ricker,	12	48	½	½		1	1¼				1		1½		1		
Sarah J Rollins,	16	48	1	1		1	1		1½	1			2		1		
Lucy J Ross,	13	48	3		1	2	1		1½		1½					1	
Angenette Stickney,	15	42	2½		5	2	1½		1½	1			1½				
Fannie C Wendell,	13	48	1		4	1½	1	1					2	1	1½		
Susan H Whitehouse,	17	48	4½	3½		1	1	1			1		1½				
Eliza E B Whitehouse,	15	48	10		3	2	1½		2	1½						3	
Laura A Wentworth,	16	7	3														
Harriet N Woodward,	18	48	6			1	1¼		1½	1	1½					1	

Whole number of Scholars entered, 63—33 Boys, 30 Girls. Of this number 5 attended less than two weeks

The highest rank in Recitations and Deportment is denoted by the figure 1; the lowest by 6.—2 is very good; 3 is respectable; below 3 is not very creditable.

J. T. FURBER, Printer.

A Great Falls High School report card of 1854. This report card, issued only four years after the high school opened, shows ages ranging from eleven to nineteen. The curriculum included not only such basics as arithmetic, history, and Latin, but also French, physiology, natural philosophy, and deportment.

The above photograph is of the original high school of Somersworth. Opened in 1850, it was claimed to be the oldest public high school in the state. It was located at the top of "the hill" overlooking the city, which gave way to the nickname, "The Hilltoppers." It was torn down in 1927 to make way for a new high school (pictured below) with greater space. This building served as the high school until 1956 when the current high school was completed. It still serves the city as the Hilltop Elementary School.

The Burliegh School. This elementary school, also known as the Orange Street School, was erected at the corner of Orange Street (Constitutional Way) and Washington Street in 1874. It was torn down in the mid-twentieth century. Its most remarkable feature was its interesting architecture, which included separate doors for boys and girls.

Children in a snowy street in Berwick. Handwriting on the picture reads, "Rochester Street, Berwick, ME., winter." Life across the river in Berwick was much the same as in Somersworth. Notice that the streets were not plowed, but the sidewalk has been cleared to allow safer walking.

A view of some of the residential streets of Somersworth. Most of the land on the hills overlooking the downtown area was residential. Behind these trees on High and Prospect Streets, the houses are large, indicating the status of the owners. Here the managers, merchants, and other prosperous people lived.

Not far from town and the residential streets were many small farms. The above photograph is of a family farmhouse and outbuildings, while in the photograph below Ernest Foss sits on his "homemade" tractor at his family farmhouse on Green Street, *c.* 1940.

Tenement buildings. Not everybody in town lived in residential homes or farmhouses. Many mill workers lived in private or company-owned boarding houses and tenements like the two pictured here. Although the boarding houses have been torn down, a few tenements survive.

School Street in Berwick. As in Somersworth, the area surrounding downtown Berwick was primarily residential. Notice the wagon ruts in the dirt road.

The entrance to Forest Glade Cemetery. Dedicated *c.* 1850, Forest Glade still serves as the city's main cemetery. Like many cemeteries of that time, it served not only as a final resting place but was also a peaceful, landscaped spot on the edge of town ideal for weekend strolls.

An exterior view of the Highland Sanitarium. Opened on August 1, 1888, the sanitarium on the top of Prospect Hill was a place "specially designed for the treatment of surgical and medical cases in the city of Somersworth." The term "sanitarium" refers to what we today would call a hospital. This was meant to serve both public and private needs with "modern comforts and conveniences including a large tent provided with hammocks and chairs, offering a cool, shady, and delightfully quiet nook for convalescents."

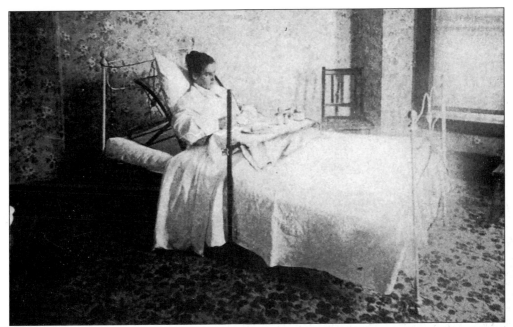

A patient at the Highland Sanitarium. According to a Highland Sanitarium pamphlet, "Every effort has been made to eliminate as far as possible the displeasing features of a large hospital, and provide for the sick a quiet, homelike and comfortable retreat...Every bed is supplied with an electric bell communicating with an anunciator in the dining room, a woven wire bolster and an invalids table and book rack, thus contributing much to the comfort and convenience of patients."

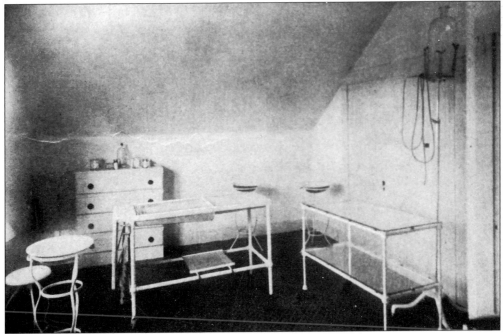

The operating room at the Highland Sanitarium, which was equipped with the best furniture and appliances for the application of the principles of modern surgery."

A view of the Salmon Falls River and the Somersworth Pumping Station, looking north. The Somersworth Pumping Station was located just north of downtown, off Rocky Hill Road. Its original function was to pump water from the river to the water tower at the top of Prospect Hill. For many years prior to World War II, the building lay vacant—Somersworth's water was supplied by wells. After World War II, the building was used as a tool and dye shop. Today the city's water is once again pumped from the river at the water treatment plant at this same site.

The Somersworth Pumping Station.

Four

Spend and Deliver

Any successful downtown requires successful stores and businesses. Many stores in Somersworth were locally owned and operated, but chain stores did make an appearance, including Woolworth's 5 & 10, Bon Marche, and the Boston Clothing Company. These stores provided local residents with all they needed, from clothes and dry goods to watches and jewelry to harnesses, lace, and tropical fruit. A trip to downtown was a chance to buy from the latest shipment from Boston and the rest of the world. The stores shown in the following pages represent almost one hundred years of shopping and business in Somersworth. The names have changed frequently over the years, as have the goods sold. With the advent of the car, the need for leather horse harnesses diminished, just as the modern department stores have eliminated the need to buy all "dry-goods" downtown. Somersworth is actually more fortunate than some mill cities because its downtown has survived the passing of the mills and is still a vital part of the city.

Grampa Nelson. Joseph Nelson came to Somersworth from Italy, settling here in 1885. He operated this Market Street store from the early 1890s to 1898. He bought his fruit from Boston, but made candy, "smokes," and ice cream himself.

The F.W. Woolworth & Co. 5 and 10 Cent Store, c. 1913. From the turn of the century and throughout much of the twentieth century the five-and-dime, chains of low-priced department stores, served the public in small towns around America. This photo shows women workers and a wonderful display of bright and shiny pots and pans.

Florence Provencher Landry at her shop located at 103 Main Street, *c.* 1910. Lace items displayed in the windows were probably handmade by Mrs. Landry. This shop was later occupied by A.G. Landry, who sold tobacco and confectioneries.

Hanson & York. This business was located at the corner of Green and Washington Streets in the area where the Free Will Baptist Church would later be built. The barrel on the sign indicates the type of business. Barrels had many uses, carrying everything from food to nails. There is quite a contrast between these men in their overalls and the fine goods available at Mrs. Landry's.

The interior of an unknown drugstore. This store seemed to have all the necessities of life, from seeds to chocolate to cosmetics. The "couple" in the back is actually part of the display. Unlike modern "self-service" stores, the goods were kept behind the counter and you were waited on by the storekeeper.

Mr. Hirsch at Hirsch's Store. Carl Hirsch operated this store on Market Street in the former Woolworth's building from the 1930s to the 1970s. He carried anything you could possibly want, if only you could find it. You may not have known how to find your way through the jumble but he knew exactly where everything was and could find it for you in an instant.

A Krisp-Nut truck and advertisement. Another Somersworth original, the Krisp-Nut Machine was invented by Somersworth native Adelard Deschesnes. Among the enticements to buy your own machine were: "Sold on easy time payments. It earns its cost several times in a year"; "200% profit. No Waste. No Shrinkage"; "Time is money do not waste valuable time by cooking nuts by hand"; and "Eating salted nuts becomes a habit when cooked in a Krisp-Nut Machine."

Krisp-Nut Machine Co.

Somersworth, New Hampshire

The J.J. Woodward Watch & Jewelry Establishment. Somersworth had many small stores up through the 1960s. These included not only dry goods stores but also jewelry stores and photographers.

The Steam Printing House in 1888. Located at the corner of High and Beacon Streets, this building was probably built in the 1840s. The *Great Falls Journal and Advertiser* was printed here from 1867 to 1881 when it was bought out by the *Free Press*. The building was torn down in 1888 to widen the road and make travel down Beacon Street safer.

The interior of the Print Shop. Before our modern age of mass production and computer images, print-making was important to making art available to society.

J.W. Bates & Co., Shoes and Leather Goods. This leather goods store not only provided the city with shoes and boots but also other necessities of that age, such as the harnesses displayed on the table in front of the store.

A Boston Clothing House advertisement from December of 1896. Victorian advertisements were decorative and fanciful. Rather than display the items to be sold, businesses often chose images such as children or animals to sell their products.

A. Wimpfheimer & Bros. This was a dry goods store on the first floor of the Great Falls Hotel building.

The George Moore Store. This was another small store downtown. Before the days of automobiles and malls, shopping was done in small local stores and "going to town" was the high point of the week.

A W.A. Moore & Son advertisement. Here is another example of Victorian advertising. Can you tell what this is advertising?

Cascade Steam Laundry. Located on High Street, this building also housed a butcher shop. When was the last time laundry was delivered? The styles tell their own story.

A.E. Ouellette Dry & Fancy Goods, c. 1905. This shop was located on Main Street across from the railroad depot. This float was made at a time when parades and celebrations meant something different than they do today. The car is a Stanley Steamer, seen here in front of the Bon Marche building; it had to be cranked underneath to start it.

Five

Meeting Places

Throughout the ages, people have always had certain places where they have gathered together to worship, to play, and to share their lives. Within Somersworth and the surrounding areas there are a number of these meeting places. Religion has always been important to Somersworth, a town which was formed as a parish of the Congregational church. When the mills began to grow and the center of town began to migrate to Great Falls, one of the first meeting places to move was the church itself. As more people came to town, more churches appeared and the Congregational church was no longer the official church of the town. Beyond the churches there were other places that people could meet as well: some people preferred to see plays at the local theater, while others chose to join social clubs or organizations. Whatever people were looking for they could probably find in Somersworth. The following photographs will show you some of the different places where family and friends have gathered over the years.

The Holy Trinity Church and Rectory. In 1859 the Holy Trinity Church was the first catholic church built in Somersworth. Located on Main Street near the corner of Indigo Hill Road, the church was torn down July 16, 1964, after being deemed unsafe by the city. Directly behind the church on Indigo Hill Road was the parochial school, which remained a catholic school into the early 1970s. A new church was built in a more spacious location on High Street in the mid-1960s.

The Free Will Baptist Church. This church, dedicated in 1842 as the Free Will Baptist Church, was located at the corner of Green and Washington Streets. The building was sold to the Greek Orthodox church, Assumption of the Virgin Mary in 1920. Today it serves as elderly housing.

The interior of the United Baptist Church. Located on High Street across from Fore Street (near the Somersworth Savings Bank), this church was above a store front. It was torn down in the 1970s.

The interior of St. Martin's Church, during the dedication of the Carillon, 1929. Constructed between 1889–90, this was the favored church of the French-Canadian immigrants. Like Holy Trinity and other traditional catholic churches, the interiors were ornate and beautiful. When the bells were dedicated in 1929 parishioners could give a donation to ring them. The bells were eventually placed in the bell tower, and when the building was torn down they were moved to the tower of the new church on West High Street.

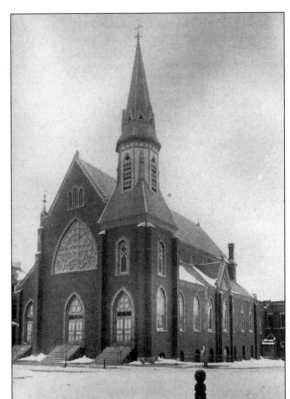

St. Martin's Church and Academie. At its location on the corner of Green and Franklin Streets, this church served its parishioners until it was closed in 1970 due to deteriorating conditions. Although the church building was torn down, its school and rectory currently serve as the Charpentier Apartments.

PRIEZ

POUR LE REPOS DE L'AME DE

REV. CLEOPHAS DEMERS

Curé de St. Martin de Somersworth, N. H.

Né le 7 novembre 1847, ordonné prêtre le 4 mars 1872, décédé à Somersworth, N. H., le 12 août 1906.

Il a beaucoup travaillé pour le Seigneur.
[Rom. XVI, 12.

Toute l'assemblée des saints racontera ses aumônes.
[Eccl. XXXI, 11.

Souvenez-vous de ceux qui vous ont prêché la parole de Dieu et imitez leur foi.
[Hebr. XIII, 7.

O bon Jésus, donnez-lui le repos éternel.
(7 ans et 7 quar. d'ind.)
R. I. P.

A funeral card for the Reverend Cleophas Demers, born November 7, 1847, and ordained March 4, 1872. He was the first pastor of St. Martin's and served the parish until his death on August 12, 1906.

Father Demer's funeral procession. The adoration for this beloved figure in the community is evident by the size of the procession for his funeral. The line of carriages stretches out of sight in the distance down Main Street. On the street are citizens in their "Sunday best" who have come to pay their last respects.

The monument of Father Desrosiers. Father Desrosiers was the pastor of St. Martin's from 1907 to 1926. He followed Father Demers, and like his predecessor, the French community marked his passing with honor and grandeur.

Salmon Falls Episcopal Church. The Protestant Episcopal church was established in 1830. For the first year they met wherever they could until the church building was built in 1831.

The Methodist Episcopal Church in Berwick. This scene shows the Berwick Methodist Episcopal Church as it appeared in the 1880s at its site on School Street.

The St. Marys Catholic Church in Salmon Falls. This Roman Catholic church was built in 1857 near the passenger railroad station in Salmon Falls. St. Mary's parish still serves the catholic population of Rollinsford.

The Salmon Falls Congregational Church. When "Summersworth" separated from Dover in 1729 it became a separate parish of the Congregational church. The center of that parish community was where Rollinsford Junction is today. As the mills developed, Salmon Falls and Great Falls developed their own congregations, and the 1st Congregational Society in Great Falls was formed in 1827.

The Furber Memorial Chapel. This chapel was erected in 1897 at a cost of $10,000. It was dedicated to James Thomas Furber (who was for many years the manager of the Boston and Maine Railroad) and his wife, Jane Roberts Furber, by their daughter Lizzie Jane Poor.

The Great Falls Hotel. This prominent downtown landmark was built in 1825 by the Great Falls Manufacturing Company. It was not uncommon for manufacturing companies to build and operate hotels. The first manager here was the cousin of poet John Greenleaf Whittier, who was an occasional guest at the hotel.

Knights of Columbus members in front of their new hall. In the early 1900s the Knights of Columbus bought and renovated the Great Falls Hotel for use as a meeting hall. Located where the present day police station is, this building had street fronts on both High and Main Streets. This group photograph of the Knight of Columbus was taken in front of the High Street entrance during renovations. In the heyday of the hotel, the Main Street side featured many stores on the first floor.

The Knights of Columbus Hall. Here we see the exterior and interior of completed hall.

The fire at the Knights of Columbus Hall on March 12, 1933, was probably the worst fire in the city's history. Not only did the fire completely destroy the hall, but many of the other buildings on the block as well. The building is shown here from the Main Street side.

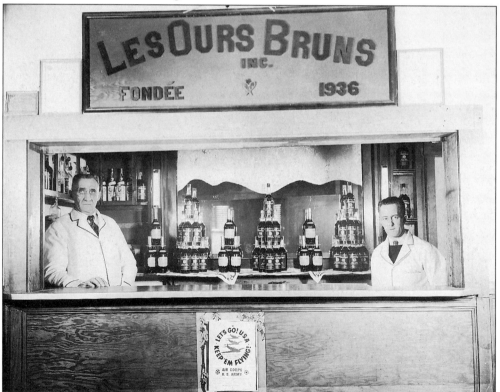

Les Ours Bruns in 1942. Founded in 1936, this social club was a popular gathering spot for many of the city's French-Canadian men. Pictured here are Adolphe Lapointe Sr. and Mr. Brissard. Note the World War II support poster.

Opera House and Main Street, Somersworth, N. H.

#21 (56) The Somersworth Opera House. Constructed in 1846 at a cost of $4,000, the Opera House was originally a plain building intended more for use as a town meeting hall than for entertainment. This changed with the remodelling in 1899, when the Opera House, or Somersworth Theater, became the home of shows, plays, and later, movies. Pictured below are the theater balconies; notice the ornate dome ceiling.

The interior of the Opera House. This view shows the gilded and lavish stage. Behind the stage and velvet curtains was an ocean scene hand-painted in bright blues and greens.

The interior of the Opera House during the Clerks Ball, 1911. The Opera House was not only home to performances but also to balls and special events. Here we see the same stage as above decorated for the Clerks Ball. Once again, the presence of the mills can be felt in this photograph.

The Opera House fire. The Opera House was destroyed by arson on February 24, 1966. It was slated to be demolished as part of the Urban Renewal project that effected much of the area. The fire was especially hard to fight due to the horrible conditions that night. Chunks of burning debris as large as footballs fell as temperatures neared 16 below zero, and high winds carried sparks as far as Rollinsford. The serenity of the sun glittering off the ice in the bottom photograph contrasts the destruction of the previous night. The remains of this building and many surrounding it were soon leveled during the Urban Renewal project.

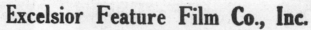

Excelsior Feature Film Co., Inc.

PRESENTS

OCTAVIA HANDWORTH

— IN —

The Path Forbidden

From the book by John B. Hymer
IN FIVE PARTS

(Issued through Alliance Films Corporation.)

Also the Latest Essanay Chaplin Comedy	FEATURED AT THE **Somersworth Theatre** **Wednesday, Nov. 17th.** Doors open at 7.30. Show at 8.	Also the Latest Essanay Chaplin Comedy

Featuring Charlie Chaplin in "Shanghaied" in 2 Reels

A flyer for *The Path Forbidden.* This flyer is advertising one of the many films that were shown at the Somersworth Theatre until it closed its doors.

Six

From Here to There and Back Again

When Somersworth began there were two forms of transportation: by horse or by foot. Transportation has changed a great deal since the eighteenth century, and it has become part of our everyday life. We sometimes forget the importance and impact of modern transportation upon us: without it we would have much less contact with the outside world, and we would be unable to get products from outside our immediate vicinity or to get our products to outside markets. Who would have thought that a city the size of Somersworth, in rural New Hampshire, would have a major train station or a trolley running through it? If we look carefully in these photographs we can see not only the major changes that brought us from the horse and buggy to the automobile, but all the variations along the way. In examining these photographs, it is easy to imagine how different our lives would be today without the convenience of modern transportation.

The Boston & Maine Railroad Station. In the days before the railroad came to town, all freight had to be hauled overland up High Street to Dover. The Boston and Maine Railroad Station formally opened on July 4, 1843, and the first train arrived "amid the booming of cannons, firing of crackers, barking of dogs and a general hurrah of the people" (*History of Stafford County*, 249). The first railroad station (pictured above) had two waiting corridors, one for men and one for women. It was removed in 1886 to make way for a more modern station in 1887 which is still standing and currently home to local restaurants. The steam engine on the right was the *Medford* and for a 10¢ fare it carried passengers from Great Falls to Rollinsford and other connecting lines to Boston from 1845–1876. The *Medford* was one of the few all steam engines that ever ran regular routes in New Hampshire. One of the members of the Somersworth Historical Society recalls, "a train trip, long or short was an event, and we made the most of it."

The Salmon Falls Train Station. Rollinsford had two railroad stations, one at Salmon Falls village (pictured above) and one at Rollinsford Junction. The line at Rollinsford Junction had a branch track to Great Falls, and it connected with the Great Falls and Conway Railroad to go north.

This is the train bridge between Rollinsford and South Berwick. Here the Boston & Maine crossed the Salmon Falls River and the state line on its way to Portland.

For hundreds of years horses and wagons supplied the daily transportation needs of the public and businesses alike. Roads made carriage and freight travel fast and smooth for the day. The first road in Great Falls, laid out in 1755, began at the corner of what is now Prospect and Main and ran over Prospect Hill and eventually into Dover. That was the only road to Dover until 1823, when what is now High Street was built. This was followed in 1837 with Green Street. It was at this time, with the growth of the mill, that many of the other roads downtown came into existence. Horses and wagons, like the Local Express Wagon (above) and the one pictured below, linked people to the outside world.

These children from the Great Falls Woolen Company tenements are being transported to school. How about this for a school bus? Crowded and cold, these company kids are still simply kids: just take a look at those faces.

Fancy horses, wagons, and cars, c. 1904. This Old Home Day event shows the transition from horses to "horseless carriages." At this time, which was not so long ago, cars were a new thing and not immediately embraced by all. Of course, not all cars were as unique as this one.

Early trolleys in Somersworth. The Electric Street Railway came to Somersworth in 1890. The first run started at Burgett's (Central) Park and continued to Great Falls via the newly constructed line on High Street. At the turn of the century trolley runs were scheduled nearly every half hour from 5:35 am to 10:35 pm. The trolley made travel between towns fast, easy, and inexpensive, but cars would soon make trolleys obsolete. The tracks were torn up in 1926.

Somersworth Trolley line #3 in snow on High Street. It may be surprising that there were trolleys in Somersworth, but there was a point when even remote towns often had trolleys. In fact, at one time you could ride all over New England on the lines. Trolleys were so commonplace in Somersworth that children used them to ride to school. As one of the members of the Somersworth Historical Society recalls: "I rode to school on #3. The city used to give us tickets to ride the streetcar to get to school."

A trolley snow plow. Trolleys needed to run year-round and this presented certain problems. In the old days, snow-covered roads were rolled and traveled on sleighs, but trolleys needed the snow plowed out of the way to have the tracks cleared for travel.

A Higley Unicycle, *c.* 1895. Famed local inventor Eben Higley patented this unique form of transportation on June 18, 1895. It weighed 60 Q w pounds, was 7' 3" high, and had a 2 inch pneumatic tire. The rider is W.P. Wilmont of Fall River.

Seven

Play Time

Amusement and recreation: what would our lives be like without them? Throughout the years people have come together to watch and play sports, to see shows and concerts, and to take Saturday afternoon trips together. Over the years recreation has followed many popular trends. In the late 1800s strolls and carriage rides in the country were the favorite pastime for Sunday afternoons. Around the turn of the century, popular activities included memberships in many different kinds of organizations, especially in tennis, bicycle, and photography clubs. Plays and trips to the park for a concert, ball game, or a picnic were also extremely popular at this time. With the advent of automobiles in the early twentieth century, day trips expanded to include popular vacation spots like the beaches or the White Mountains. Although some of these amusements are still popular today, many have faded away and been replaced by video games and rented movies, while the Sunday afternoon stroll has become the trip to the mall.

The players, on February 8, 1921. These actors are preparing for a community show at the Great Falls Hotel. Community plays such as this one were popular throughout the late 1800s and the early part of this century.

A Somersworth tennis tournament in August of 1889. The Somersworth Tennis Club courts on Paige Street were built in the 1880s and existed well in to the 1920s. Tennis clubs were commonplace around the turn of the century, as were other sports clubs. These courts were located not far from the Toboggan Club's run. Note the fashions of the day and the undeveloped land beyond the courts.

Tennis players gather at a home on Paige Street. What to do after the game? These players are gathered at what is believed to be the home of Bessie Freeman. Others identified in this party are Mr. & Mrs. Carter (who owned a dry goods store that would later become Hirsch's), Mr. Frederick Ricker of Berwick, and Miss Emery of Prospect Street.

The Somersworth High School football team of 1898. Here we have the stylish young gentlemen of a team of one hundred years ago. Uniforms, shoes, and even the ball are different, including the noticeable lack of padding and helmets.

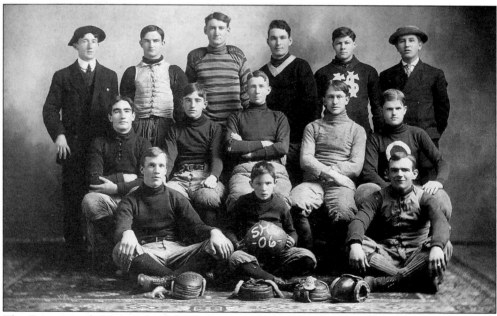

The Somersworth High School football team of 1906. It is only eight years after the above photograph, and styles have already changed. At least now there are helmets, sort of. From left to right are: (top row) Shanahan (Manager), O'Wallier, Moran, W. Hanagan, Flanagan, and Nolette; (second row) R. Hanagan, Riley, Foss, Hobart, and Pray; (front row) Miles, Conley (mascot), and Keer.

The Somersworth High School baseball team of 1906. This was the most successful team in the school's history to that point. They had a record of 13 wins out of 16 games and won the state championship. Standing with the team is Principal Ferguson, in the center.

The Somersworth High School baseball team of 1933. Things can certainly change in thirty years. The team is posed in front of the new high school. Certain basic elements such as mitts look much more like their 1900 counterparts than those of today.

The Somersworth High School basketball team. The shoes sure are along cry from Air Jordans, and when was the last time you saw buckles on a basketball uniform?

The pool hall on Main Street. Children walking by this pool hall were told by their parents "to look down and turn their eyes away as they passed."

Joe St. Hillaire. Joe was possibly one of the greatest boxers to ever come out of the seacoast region. In a career that spanned the twenties, Joe fought in Dover, Portsmouth, and Boston, bringing home many victories along the way.

Boxer Emil "Young" Gauvin was remembered by one member of the Somersworth Historical Society as, "The only cop in town, and let me tell you, the kids behaved. He'd let you get in the first shot, but that was it!"

Amos Foss was the manager and drummer of this and later bands such as the Bay View Pavillion Orchestra; he would also eventually become the superintendent of the Great Falls Bleachery and Dye Works. Also in the above photograph are, from left to right: John Adams, Frank Perry, Herby Ayers, Amos Foss, Ellis Hemingway, Teles Perreault, and Freddie Vallee. Amos Foss and his orchestra played at various halls in New Hampshire and Maine throughout the first half of the century. The bottom photograph is a Metronome Dance Orchestra business card, c. 1927.

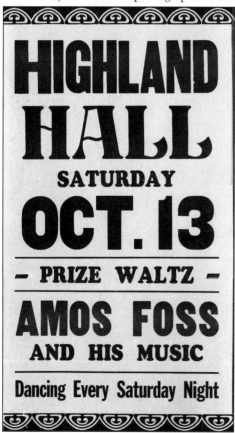

Somersworth bands in the early twentieth century. The Somersworth City Band was formed in 1908. The city was home to many bands throughout the years including the Vixen Independent Drum Corps and also bands from the Veterans of Foreign Wars and the Knights of Columbus. Bands provided entertainment at many community functions and parades.

A drawing of Central Park at the turn of century (above), with the Dover, Somersworth, and Rochester street railway depot (below). Central Park was located away from the downtown on the shores of Willand Pond, with 69 acres in Somersworth and 4 acres in Dover, in the area that today is across from Tri-City Plaza. It was laid out in 1890 by H.W. Burgett, an agent acting for the Consolidated Light and Power Company and the Union Street Company, both trolley companies. Trolley companies built several amusement areas throughout New England on their lines, providing working class people with affordable entertainment and a means of getting there.

The bandstand and monkey cage at Central Park. Central Park not only had evening concerts from the bandstand but it had animals in a monkey cage and a bear cage, as well as ball fields, dances, and picnic areas.

The bear cage at Central Park. Today all that remains of this turn-of-the-century park is the remnants of the bear cage.

The Central Park Casino and Lake. Central Park had a casino and theater for communities functions. The theater had a capacity of 2,000 people with every seat in full view of the stage. Though most of the park faded away over time, the theater continued to show movies well into the middle of this century.

Esmeralda was presented by the Berwick Grange in December of 1908. This production shows the close tie between the three communities on the Salmon Falls River. It concerns a family in North Carolina and Paris, and featured vocal, violin, and trombone solos and vaudeville.

Eight
Special Events

Today's Fourth of July fireworks and Memorial Day parades are two remnants of the pomp and celebration that community events often held for towns as recently as the 1960s. A holiday celebration meant more than a simple family gathering—it was a full day of events with a parade starting the day that the whole town turned out for. Parades were often followed by big community barbecues or special performances of community plays. One of the biggest events of the summer in the first years of this century was "Old Home Week," featuring parades with banners and streamers draped across houses and stores. Somersworth took great pride in these events, as is apparent by the following photographs. The city still takes pride in its special events, including the annual Children's Festival, which takes place throughout the downtown area: it is a modern day reminder of the pageant and gala of former community events.

A view of Main Street during a late-1800s Fourth of July celebration. It seems as if the whole town has turned out, and Main Street is full of spectators; we can only guess what the performers were doing. In many places the Fourth of July was one of the few days that the mills were closed.

The Somersworth Post Office during World War I, *c.* 1917. The sign reads "Christmas gifts from teachers and schoolchildren for the Somersworth boys somewhere in France. Have you sent your gift? Have you done your bit?" Fourth-grade schoolchildren knitted squares to make quilts to send to soldiers; other gifts were items like toothpaste and toothbrushes.

The Preparedness Parade of Berwick, Maine, *c.* 1917. Large and small towns around the nation showed support and prepared for the First World War, as can be seen here in this parade in Sullivan Square.

Old Home Days and the Fourth of July always provided opportunities for community events and parades. The above photograph is of a late-nineteenth-century parade with a decorated tool wagon on Market Street, while the photograph below is of a parade in Rollinsford. Parades, then as now, included many community groups and local businesses.

Republican headquarters in Great Falls, *c.* 1888. Elections were more than politics; they were also a special event. Below is the Harrison and Morton Drum Corps. In this view we can see this "log cabin" is actually downtown on Main Street, sitting in front of the mill and across the street from the mill boarding houses.

Memorial Hall on High Street. Dedicated in 1888, this is the Memorial Hall of the Grand Army of the Republic, a business and social center for Veterans of the Civil War. The second floor contained business and meeting rooms and the ground floor contained reading and billiard rooms. This gathering of soldiers was likely taken during the dedication; behind the banner is the partially hidden poster of the face of President Harrison.

The Stephen J. Wentworth Camp, No. 14, of the Sons of Veterans. Stephen J. Wentworth was a Somersworth resident killed during the Civil War. This unit was for sons of Union veterans. This photograph indicates the pomp and patriotism so much a part of the late nineteenth century.

Nine

City People

City life has always been more than just buildings and mills and work: cities were where people gathered, played, and lived. In previous chapters we have seen what they did for recreation and special events; in this chapter we will see residents at moments of frolic and ease. These photographs could have been taken not only in Somersworth, but almost anywhere in America at the turn of the century, and they represent not only this city but the country at that time as a whole. In many ways it is the people of any age that let us really feel what it was like to live in that age. In their eyes, faces, and fashions we can catch a glimpse of how they lived and what was important to them.

A lobster feed at the beach. This photograph of an outing to the beach shows some of the mill management, including Cy Freeman, Charles Plummer (the agent), Les Faunce (the undertaker), and who could miss the proud lobster man!

The St. Hillaire Bottler picnic. This local family-run bottler of soda became the Coca-Cola Bottler in 1916. Coca-Cola continued in the city until the 1980s.

Snowshoers. This moment of frivolity shows a popular activity of the turn of the century. This photograph includes Bessie Freeman, a teacher at the Burliegh School and daughter of Cy Freemen, who was the overseer of the cloth room.

A day at the beach. At the turn of the century, with the increased availability of transportation and leisure time, Americans began to make trips and excursions more commonplace. A popular destination was the beach. It must have been tough to get a tan in those suits!

Because of the initial limitations of photography, most photographs were posed and not the candid snapshots of today. This applied to formal portraits and shots in the home. Even so, these photographs show some clever poses. The above shot in a Victorian home gives a good sample of the decoration and style of the day. The photograph to the right shows young people in turn-of-the-century fashions.

The photograph above is of the wedding of
Archie St. Laurent and Rose Beaupre in the late
1920s. Below is the wedding picture of the
oldest son of Peter Gagne, a local photographer.
Weddings are important celebrations in any age
and these photographs are a celebration of
wedding fashions. How many modern day brides
go off to their honeymoon in a bearskin coat?

A man with many flags. This collection of flags of the world could have been gathered for any number of reasons. The flag of Israel indicates that this is a post-1947 photograph.

J.T.C. women. This is most likely a portrait of a late-nineteenth-century temperance group, perhaps the Junior Temperance Club. Notice the oriental rug, apparently the same one seen in many of the other portraits so far. Pictured here are, from left to right: (back row) Laura Ross, Minnie Perreault, Clementine Doyon, Laura Doyon, Demarise Pageotte Bernier, and Leah Jacques; (second row) Alice Ruel, Leonie Perreault Labissoniere, and Alma Roy; (front) unknown, and Eva Ross.

Two group photographs of well-dressed men. The bottom picture is composed of everyone who happened to be on the scene when the photographer arrived. They included, from left to right: (back row) Jim Locke, Sam Davis, Print Pierce, Mr. Marston, Phil Stiles, Joe Libby, and Charles Smith; (middle) Cy Freeman, Mr. Thurston, Charles Worster, and Mr. Kimball; (bottom) Ben Bragdon, Hart Chapman, Arthur Bailey, Pardon Dexter, and Eugene Hawes. While the picture above is quite possibly not related to the mill, the bottom is definitely a gathering of mill personnel. The stars on the wall behind these men, though decorative, perform an important function and act to brace mill building against the movement of the machines inside.

Local actors, in a post-World War II photograph. Although this looks like a family gathering, in reality this is the cast of local play. Included in this photo is Doc Adams, a leading physician in town who delivered many town residents. Is it Hoody Doody time?

Four people on the stoop of a house. Photographs serve many purposes, and it is difficult to tell whether this photograph was intended to be more of the house or of the family. In either case it has preserved the moment in time beautifully.

The style of the day in the late 1800s. Above is an unknown man dressed in high fashion for a special occasion. You've got to love that cape. In the photograph below everyday men pose casually in casual clothes, much different than the jeans and t-shirts of today.

Stages and auditoriums were an important part of the community, and were used as locations for plays and performances, lectures, and exhibitions. This photograph is of the Rollinsford Auditorium in the 1920s. The Rollinsford Town Hall housed an auditorium on the second floor. Notice the rolled carpet behind these men and the heavy curtains of the stage.

A group of women actors hamming it up for the photographer.

Ten

A Tour of Somersworth
Then and Now

Many people have visited Somersworth over the years. Some were just passing through on their way north, others were visiting family and friends, and still others came to see the mills. We thought that it would be nice to end this book with a tour of old Somersworth, a tour that a visitor to the city may have taken a hundred years ago. Most of the buildings here are bedecked with banners and flags. They are dressed up for "Old Home Week," one of the city's biggest celebrations around the turn of the century. You will find that many of these scenes have changed very little today; it makes us wonder what the city will look like one hundred years from now.

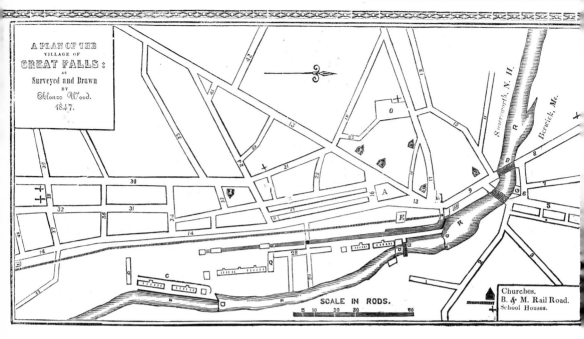

EXPLANATIONS TO THE ABOVE PLAN.

A, Central Buildings. B, Great Falls Bank. C, Canals. D, Post Office. E, Boston and Maine Rail Road Depot. B, in river, Bridges. D, in river, Dams. G, Rollins' Steam Mill. I, W. E. Griffin & Co.'s Iron Foundry. J, Methodist church. K, Evangelical Baptist church. L, Universalist church. M, Congregational church. N, Old Freewill Baptist church. O, Cemetery. P, Town Hall. Q, Cotton Houses. Y, New Freewill Baptist church.

1, ADAMS COURT.	12, MOUNT WASHINGTON STREET.	23, ELM STREET.	35, PLEASANT STREET.
2, BERWICK STREET.	13, CENTRAL SQUARE.	24, WASHINGTON STREET.	36, FRANKLIN STREET.
3, NORTH STREET.	14, MAIN STREET.	25, COURT STREET.	37, SPRING STREET.
4, BACK STREET.	15, HIGH STREET.	27, MIDDLE LANE.	38, PINE STREET.
5, SULLIVAN STREET.	16, FORE STREET.	28, CANAL STREET.	39, SOUTH STREET.
6, BOW STREET.	17, PROSPECT STREET.	29, CANAL COURT.	40, SOUTH SUMMER STREET.
7, NORTH SUMMER STREET.	18, PARKS STREET.	30, GREEN STREET.	41, MECHANIC'S STREET.
8, BRIDGE STREET.	19, WESTERN AVENUE.	31, BROAD STREET.	42, ROCHESTER STREET.
9, MARKET STREET.	20, CEMETERY LANE.	32, UNION STREET.	43, ROAD TO NEW FACTORIES
10, NORTH UNION STREET.	21, ORANGE STREET.	33, CHURCH STREET.	ABOUT TO BE ERECTED BY THE
11, CONCORD STREET.	22, MARSTON STREET.	34, FAYETTE STREET.	G. F. M. Co.
			44, SCHOOL STREET.

An 1847 map of Great Falls. This map is an overview of the layout of the city as it looked as the mills were reaching their peak. Although many of the buildings in the city have changed, the basic street plan has changed very little since its origin. We will use this map to trace a brief tour through historic Somersworth. The tour begins as we come into Somersworth from Berwick (8); and we will then travel down Market Street (9) with a brief stop on Prospect Street (17); next, we will go up High Street (15) and end up back at the Great Falls Manufacturing Company (28).

This is a view of the new iron bridge connecting Somersworth and Berwick. A 1770 proposal to build a bridge spanning the Salmon Falls River to connect Berwick and Great Falls was turned down by the town, but in 1783 a bridge was constructed with each town paying half the upkeep. In the late 1800s a new iron bridge replaced the earlier one, and each town was still responsible for maintenance into the twentieth century. Today this continues to be the main connection between the two towns.

Market Street. As we head up Market Street the first large building we see on our left is this one, formerly the home of George Moore's Store and Dr. Hammond the dentist. Today this building still houses stores and businesses.

Market Street, *c.* 1890s. Continuing up Market Street we head further into the shopping district. The center building, with the carriages in the front, was the home of Woolworth's 5 & 10, and later Hirsch's Department Store. The scene looks remarkably similar today (minus the banners and horses).

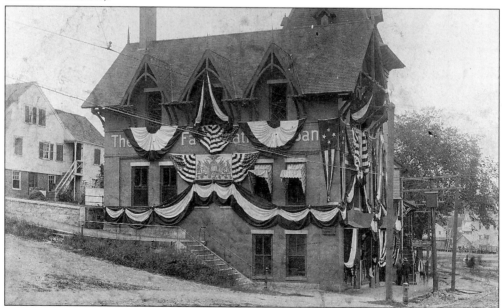

The Great Falls National Bank. Built on the site of the first blacksmith shop in Great Falls, and located at the corner of Prospect and High, the first two streets in town, this building housed banks beginning in 1846. For a number of years this building was shared by the Great Falls National Bank and the Somersworth National Bank. It continued as a bank until 1965, and today it is home to one of the best known bakeries in town.

The oldest house in Somersworth. Looking up the hill on Prospect Street, directly behind the bank building, we can see the oldest house in town, erected in 1755 by one of the town's founding fathers, Joseph Wentworth.

A photograph of Etters Photographer and the town watering trough. Proceeding up Market Street we are now at Market Square, the junction of Market, Main, and High Streets. The prominent building in the center of the block is Etters Photographer, where many of the portraits seen in this book originated. A visitor could water his horse here at the town watering trough and pickup on the latest news. For many years this area was the center for local business and trading. Next to Etters is the Boston and Maine Railroad Station, and in the background we can see the mill.

The Somersworth Savings Bank on High Street. As we leave Market Square and head up High Street we come to the large building of the Somersworth Savings Bank. It housed not only the bank but the American Express Company and many other stores and businesses. It was destroyed by fire in 1963. Today a new building houses the Somersworth Savings Bank on this site. Looking further up the street we see other businesses of High Street in buildings that still stand today.

A large house decorated for Old Home Days. Heading up any of these streets away from downtown we could find large residences like this one. Many are still standing today.

The Memorial Hall Building. Located between the business and residential sections of High Street, the Memorial Hall of the Grand Army of the Republic served for many years as the gathering place for veterans. Later it would be the meeting hall of the local Masonic chapter. It is dressed here for a special event; note the horse and rider on the roof, above the doorway.

The Great Falls Manufacturing Company, from an early view. We complete our tour on Main Street with a visit to the mill, as no tour of this city would be complete without one. This is where the story of the city began. The picturesque wooden fences and dirt roads give little indication of the growth of the city and mills to come.

Work is temporarily disrupted in the mill to pose for a photograph.

The Great Falls Manufacturing Company, Mill #1, during a typical New England winter.

Acknowledgments

The majority of the photographs included in this book are from the general collection of the Summersworth Historical Society including the collections of the following people: Doris Hayden, Phil & Irene Wentworth, John Ballentine, Mona Faucher, A.S. Landry, Lillian Roberge, Pat & Clyde Coolidge, Ernest & Dot Blaisdell, George & Ann Bickford, Bessie Freeman, Jan Rhoades, Ruby Spence, Susan & Michael Mariano, Raymond Demers, Arthur Joy, Betty Foley, Brian Tapscot, Ida Patterson, Roger Varney, Elizabeth Richardson, Gemma Bisson, Constance Polychronopoulos, Rachael Pugh, and Beatrice St. Pierre. The Rollinsford and Salmon Falls pictures appear courtesy of the Rollinsford Historic Commission and the collection of Dorothy Green.

We would like to thank: all members of the Summersworth Historical Society who assisted in identifying photographs, Aaron Sturgis, Debora Longo and the Somersworth Public Library staff (for all of their assistance), Doris Hayden, Phil Wentworth, John Ballentine, and Mona Faucher, without whom this book never would have come about.

All unidentified quotes are from various members of the Somersworth Historical Society. Other facts have come from various old newspaper articles, taken primarily from the *Somersworth Free Press*. Books used were: Martin J. Flanagan, *Passing Parade* (Somersworth, 1983); James Montgomery, *A Practical Detail of the Cotton Manufacture of the United States* (Glasgow, 1840); and John Scales, *The History of Strafford County, New Hampshire* (Chicago, 1914).